ENDS AND BEGINNINGS

Iain Crichton Smith

ENDS AND BEGINNINGS

CARCANET

Acknowledgements

Acknowledgements are due to the following: *Aberdeen University Review;* BBC; *The Listener; PEN Magazine; Poetry Society Annual; Poetry Wales; The Scotsman; The Spectator; Stand; Verse.*

First published in 1994 by
Carcanet Press Limited
208-212 Corn Exchange Buildings
Manchester M4 3BQ

A CIP catalogue record for this book
is available from the British Library.
ISBN 1 85754 093 X

The publisher acknowledges financial assistance
from the Arts Council of Great Britain

Set in 10pt Palatino by Bryan Williamson, Frome
Printed and bound in England by SRP Ltd, Exeter

Contents

Poetry   1

1
Lewis   5
The Bible   6
The Nightmare   7
Old Lady   9
As a Guest   11
As Time Draws Near   12
Funeral   14
An Old Man Praying   16
Dying Man   18
In Hospital   19
Promise   20
Dogmas   21
A Day without Dogma   22
For Roy Williamson, Folk Singer   25
In Memoriam Alexander Scott, Poet   26
The Wife Speaks   28
For Champers   29
Come, Fool   31
On the Grave an MA   32
The Will   33
The Death   35
Revenant   37
Many Years After   38
Old Lady   39
From the Mad Ward   40
The Old Lady   42
In Glasgow   48
Nurses   50
The Stranger   51
Students   52
The Old Poet   53
Sometimes I Remember   54
For Livingstone, the Explorer   55

2
London   59
Turkey   60
Malta   64

On the Golan Heights   66
London   67
Aberdeen   68
Silver   69

3
The Well   73
The Song   74
I Remember   75
Teachers   77
Aberdeen   78
Putting out the Ashes   79
Christmas Tree   80
Santa Claus   81
Hallowe'en   82
Macbeth and the Witches   83
The Cuckoo   84
The Fence   85
The Spider   86
Early Spring   87
Welcome   88
The Gaelic Proverb   89
You   90
Aunt   92
Shakespeare   93
Escape   94
The Theft of the Vases   95
Two Pieces   96
Stones   97
On a Clear Day   98
Waiting for the Ferry   99
A Story   100

4
The Poet   103
No Muses   104
At a Poetry Reading   106
Compulsory Retirement   108
Milton   110
The Scholar   111
The Scholar Says Goodbye   112
Dream   113
The Young Girls   115

Tutorial   116
Books   117

5
Others   121
Leaving   122
In the Evening   124
Autumn   125
Hiding   126
Insomnia   127
The Rose Tree   128
In Aberdeen   129
For Donalda   130
In the Hospital   131
Air Hostesses   132
Capricorn   133
To a Young Scottish Poet of the Future   135

6
Conversion   141

Poetry

Poetry has nothing to do with who we are.
It cannot be explained by biography,
e.g. sickness, unhappiness.
Poetry is a swart planet
with which we are in touch, from which
we receive at certain times messages.
Nor is it a black or emerald clock –
I think it is a voice which speaks to us
at night as unquiet trembling, or maybe
a curious arrangement of stones,
poorly random and yet sonorous,
a packet of crisps beside a Greek vase
on a day with a breeze flowing from the south.

Lewis

The waves
are perversely sparkling
in'front of your house.
It is an autumn day
over bare Lewis.
Canada is far away
with your early odyssey
on the lakes
and the rivers of British Columbia.
Your Bible
sits by your chair
and your radio is silent.
More real to you than Lewis
are the stories of Israel
colourful, eloquent.
You are a sinner
holding at night in your bed
a dialogue with God.
May he have mercy on me,
you say to the mirror
in which only your own face appears,
ravaged and sparse.
Let me enter
Your kingdom of fresh water
where the insomniac angels
constantly hover.
I have built with my own hands
this house without substance.
Everything is ashes and trash.
There's a taste in my mouth like fish,
scaly and foreign.
Here where I burn
Canada is the huge barn
of my thoughtless youth.
And the salmon
pulsing in my net are souls,
restless and populous.
And the tall magnificent spruce
are climbing to heaven
above my small rocking boat
tilting in foam.

The Bible

The Bible stands like a big rock which no one attends to.
It is a novel with murders, adulteries and fears.

It is the solid TV of our human history
and God is the eagle with human flesh in its claws.

It used to be made of marble, a statue among leaves.
Now it is a record of deaths, tribal partitions.

And its victims have black faces and its saints have batons
and their diseased ethics are undazzled by rainbows.

The Nightmare

Last night I dreamed a dreadful dream.
I was fighting in a battle, sword in hand,
and there were plungings of blades in breasts.

The chief encouraged us, on a desolate moorland.
There was trickery as between dagger and sword,
there were spots of blood on jackets.

Physical terror such as I had never known,
the hackings of noses and foreheads,
blindings in that frightening silence.

And then three men found me,
humorous, velvet-jacketed and kilted.
They smiled, seeming to offer me mercy,

but just before I woke they stabbed me
repeatedly in that desolate victory
which not even the chief survived.

And as I woke I seemed to know death,
the sword piercing me like the beak of a bird
and my breast opening to a cold eternal wind.

Among jackets, bonnets, a fury of hackings,
I found my head on the white pillow again
and gazed at my empty suits in the wardrobe,

while the moon shone like a round shield
in a window between two countries
like ice that has grown over an unowned land.

Over the unowned land of the deer and the pheasant,
of the green trees and transient skies,
of the jewel-like lochs on the moorland,

of the blue rings that we are married to
in the skies of sunset that arch the moorland
and are reflected in the Tir nan Og

of a duplicitous imagination,
where the soldier fought for an empire
that paid him in forged money,

and made him an ideal king
as he fought against himself
in a mirror of imperial complexity

and a heaviness of bronze and soil
that fell on his bony shoulders
as he starved among briny seaweed

and the milk of meagre cattle.

And so from battle to battle
from dream to reality

we have staggered into this pitiless
glare of poverty and a lost language
unless perhaps we are resurrected

like an astronomy of daffodils
changing into a yellowness of stars
that shine over us

but do not pierce us with swords
or with autumn daggers
but point in a new direction

tremblingly, originally,
like the horns of the deer
peering between the wet twigs of spring.

Old Lady

1

All your sap is thickened towards survival.
About you there is no dapple of thought.
Sometimes in the evening there's a retrieval

of old rings, old bangles. Otherwise
your tale is a stubborn root against wind.
There is no narrative in your veined eyes.

Even ice can melt and become water,
adventure. No, with bitter claws
you cling to the horned stick carved from nature,

the elegant deer's head. At night
I hear you fumbling among furniture,
for beads, ribbons, dresses, moonlit rings.

2

The sea stings. It is older than you are.
Its brine is saltier than your tears.
It is a treasury of the wandering dead.

Sometimes at sunset it looks beautiful
with its strange roses among bitter green.
And in autumn moonlight how its roads converge!

Old lady, surely we are human.
But do not shut your eyes in your blindness,
nor your nostrils nor your wrinkled ears.

The crab noses the brine in the morning.
It feels through the vibrations of its shell
the constant music of the possible.

3

The lumpy wooden ones who rose from the dead,
there have been some of those. Consider the paintings
framed in the Renaissance, and still bright.

On wooden wings they rose towards feathers,
the Dutch ones too in their sabots, from their kitchens.
On their dishes a various light shone.

The lumpy ones became angels.
They sprouted from earthly dressers towards heaven.
They left a trail of bronze chains behind

and a little dog looking towards them
as their rough heels turned golden, and their bodies
filled as with water unfathomably grave.

4
To be human is to be a river
reflecting new pictures, flowing on
deftly, imperfectly, towards the future.

Loves, ruins, weddings, rest in it,
brides with white dresses descending
raptly from clouds of the minute.

Exactly so, difficult old woman,
thorny-voiced, thorny-wristed, slow
rancours seething from your waste moon.

Indignities of the posthumous.
I love tragic heroes in the storm
profiled thriftlessly against space,

but you tick like an old clock.
Useless above the grave your gaunt face,
useless the bony chair in which you rock.

As a Guest

As a guest who troubles you by staying too long
and who is found awkwardly in rooms or studying books
aslant to the house and its usual presences
so it may be that we too feel this –

our trouble to the earth, inarticulate with age,
creating more turmoil than our lives should warrant
tremulous haunters of toilets and of bedrooms –
waiting for that definite lenient stroke.

As Time Draws Near

As time draws near
the end of our days
and the plates fall

away from our knees,
let us not be afraid
of the unsponsored dark.

Heavy grave sin
is weighing your head.
There are shining in darkness

panoramas of terror.
Each nightly picture
is God in his ire.

But for us in autumn
let the trees remind us
of our reasonable sequence,

that like birds we travel
from darkness to darkness
briefly through the hall,

where there remains
the clinking of glasses,
the redness of wine,

though we lie starkly
in our effigies
which will not rise,

pen or sword in hand.
It is an achieved grand
tableau that we leave,

say, turning at the door,
putting on a glove,
and entering the sunset's

enormous concert.
Surely that is better
than on stumbling feet

in the warmth of wetness
squalidly survive.
Live O live,

all you young ones
who take our places
in this hypothesis

of sun and cloud.
May it be with pride
we applaud your litheness

in this panorama,
this drama of our days.
O yes with pride

that we step outwards
into the darkness
closing our eyes

on the last flickering page.

It is time to let the birds migrate without anguish
through the skies of the immediate
towards a fated destination.

It is time to turn the blow lamp on dogma
and inhabit this blue.

Funeral

The wind tugged at our clothes
as your coffin was borne
out on to the empty road.

We were like crows
in the middle of the autumn day
as we trudged to the hearse

with that polished chest
in which you were at rest,
your eyes closed.

The box was slowly let down
into the prepared grave.
The tassels were thrown

on to the closed lid.
Beside us the sea
stormily glittered,

minerally coloured.
I summon to mind
my loved autumn wood

and the rowan tree
with its triumphant flourish
of temporary berries,

and all that is perfect
on the verge of its dying.
It was not in a ring

of dogma or prayer
that I felt that peace,
uniquely gracious.

It belonged to the season,
to the last passion
of dignified things,

to their replete goings
as without theory
even the folded wings

of a bird declines
into the dark,
as without cleric

or the windy volume
of protective stories
we take our measure

in a natural inventory.
He was so, he was so!
The transparent window

is always open.
And so you enter,
in the complex nature

of your own history,
and also you change
in an earth not strange

but always familiar,
and the tiny daffodil
will flourish later

out of your box
which the manipulative
oily worms unlock

as the natural colourful
flowers enthral
the fresh sea breeze.

An Old Man Praying

In the middle of the night I hear you pray.
'God be with me, soon it will be time.'
And then the clock begins its crystal chime.

Provenance of the Bible and its power!
Even so far from home you're on the rack.
The day is vain and then the night is black,

starless, without compass. 'I have sinned.'
Inside your head the scarlet whores patrol.
If only light would break, and you were Paul,

self-confident and literate. Christ was once
a boy like you, fishing for his eels.
Now he hangs from wood by his tanned heels.

The box must lock us, poisonous, corrupt.
Not charitable works can save us now,
not neighbours' fields that we in mercy ploughed.

Listen, the birds begin. Is that a cat
screeching from the shrubbery? The owl
ghosts through the village, like a wafting soul.

And the birds cheep and chirrup, interrupt
the speech of Genesis, the burning stench
of flesh at sunrise far from the cool Minch.

'Tremendous pigmy on my wooden chair
I shake and stutter. Paradise exhales
a foreign scent, as roses on salt gales.

Is larger than a street of jewellers,
the haunt of youth when drunk. I would abide
His scything rainbows with my ruinous pride.

Now it is full morning, and the larks
soar straight to heaven, pagan, bodiless.'
You rise from sheets, put on your mortal dress

while rabbits race and frolic in the dew.
'I must recall my chains are made of love.
This swollen arm is fantasy. Be brave.

The soul's exhaled like scent from rotting flesh,
and like pale herring shall outlive the mesh.'

Dying Man

Breathless and blue-lipped,
you thank God for His mercies
in a prayer you have learned
on a bare island.
How grand the face of God,
secure, imperious,
to whom you are a slave
in absolute fear and dread.

Dying, you thank God,
beating at His door
for an exact justice
though you do not hear
a high answering voice.
It is only history
that sweeps grandly on
in spite of your 'Rejoice'.

Pity shakes my heart
as at night I hear
your eloquent sleepless prayers,
endless and austere.
But only the birds of dawn
answer with their twitter,
or the continuous water
chatters among leaves.

And the window rises,
contingent and gaunt,
like a white picture
misty, indigent,
over the wet grass.
Out of the vast silence
there is no voice
to raise you from your knees.

In Hospital

Over your face is the grilled snout of the oxygen mask.
I bend down to speak to you.
You are a sick eagle outspread on the bed.
Your nose grows thinner and thinner.

Oh, how lovely the nurses are
in their objective uniforms.
Their bodies sing of youth and health
in your incontinent world.

You are gazing up at me
from that country which is adjacent to me
though you have not crossed the border
breathing heavily, dully.

It is only a short distance away,
less than from Lewis to Harris.
It is a question of darkness,
away from this precious autumn.

Someone is waiting for you with scales
and a book where your sins are registered.
It is like going to school again
for the very first time.

Your eyes tell us of it.
We are no longer in the same land.
Our eyes cross that unimaginable space.
The white nurses are still here.

Promise

'If it were not so
I would have told you,
that your thatched house

will be changed to diamond.
That out of the wind
a steady mansion

will rise, conspicuous.
Poor in your house
let the dream sustain

your lean timbers.
Oh, shut your purse
on this one promise,

that miraculous windows
will rise rose-coloured
from this thistly clump.'

Dogmas

Perfidious dogmas,
unremitting theses,
let the wild seas
blow through you

with their salt taste
and tang of seaweed
and all the dead
whose bones have been picked clean

by the fresh currents,
and let the rocks of dogma
be steadily worn down
till only the water

brilliantly sparkling
with its modern ships
flows always eastward
towards a temporary sun.

A Day without Dogma

It is a day without dogma.
The rhododendrons are growing by the roadside.
The broom is in yellow flower.

To create dogma is to create a wall
that sets a boundary to the worms,
that sets a limit to the sparkle of water,
the windows without names.

The lovers are strolling hand in hand
through the green countryside.
White clouds flow across the sky.
The scent of the flowers is in my nostrils,
foxgloves, larkspurs.
Ivy grows on walls.

In studies, sombre dogma is being created.
Huge volumes lie on glass tables.
Beards of prophets stream down gaunt cheeks.
Dogma is the defence against reality
which twinkles from water and glass.

Listen, let us remember how the dinosaur
travelled like a ladder through the world,
how the chimpanzee swings from the trees,
how there are no walls created by nature,
how the animals slide through the air
which has no name.

Blood, death, and terror.
These are what dogma creates.
Behind the hard shell of the preacher
is the heart of the trembling child
who will not submit to the flow,
meaningful, meaningless,
which the world as it is presents.

Roses, water, clouds,
you are a continual transformation.
A woman walks with a shopping bag through the daylight.
Her world is unimaginable to me.
She has crossed the horizon from the tenement
or from a cottage
on which the sun paints in the evening
a glow of vivid red.

Dogma is a measure of our inability to live.

We drive through the mirrors
of this summer day, the sheep grazing,
a horse rubbing one back leg against another,
the cows swishing their tails,
the mustard and the rape
a bright and blinding yellow.

Windscreens wink at each other. There's a smell
of rank and heavy dung.

The world is without dogma. Out of our fear
we raise ideologies.
Out of the fear of the immediate, the present,
the sleepless waterfall.
Out of the fear of the spontaneous,
the untitled contemporary,
the untheological grass
which the breeze combs back with a tenderness
which is indescribably poignant.
The terror of vision, of madness,
of the unbordered bracken and heather,
of the rat which has no scholarship,
of the weasel which pulses at the throat of the rabbit,
of the mouse whose tail dangles from the cat's mouth,
of the lark which sings without justice,
of the cloud which has no chains.

Butterflies swarming in the air,
I greet you.
As also the unflagged territory
of the buzzard,
of that sparkling air without insignia.

It is time to pull down the walls,
it is time to capture the dogmas
and bury them in the wilderness.
It is time to live in the accidents of the everyday,
the varying shuttle of April,
the red hot helmets of summer,
the haggard fadings of autumn.

It is time to let the birds migrate without enigma
through the skies of the immediate
towards a fated destination.

It is time to turn the blow lamp on dogma
and inhabit this blue.

For Roy Williamson, Folk Singer

Last night the black boat called for you,
and you entered it with your guitar.

Scotland, your friends, your music, they were all gone,
as you drifted down the river

which might have been in one of your songs.
Out of the pack of cards the ace of spades.

There comes a time when the music ceases
and when it is continued by others

but not quite the same music; that is our glory.
Nightingales sing the same song over and over again.

In this continual flow, how shall your fiddle
survive? How shall your clarsach?

It will survive but always differently
as a different text in front of future eyes.

Not your hand

nor your head nor your thought, but only this changing text
sparkling at different points along the stream

strengthening, weakening, strengthening, and perhaps
weakening again as the light falls on it

as it fell on you once when walking along a lane in May
and you drummed among the thistles the song of your own land.

In Memoriam Alexander Scott, Poet

In university you were older than me.
You had won the MC in the war.
You were a handsome tall and brilliant figure.

They seem such a long time ago,
these days of scholarship and beer,
poetry, essays and the theatre.

And later still your various lectureships.
First life then death separates us all.
No one can be a perpetual

student, however brilliant or adored.
Nevertheless I remember those rich years,
your own edited magazine, your own verse,

your academic laurels. Those fresh days
survive your death, as gold survives the dross.
Lucky for those who have such happiness

before the breath is shortened. In loved Greece
you might not climb to the Acropolis.
Athletic youth, compulsory route marches,

were bright fit memories. Shall our metre fail
if our breath fails? In wintry Glasgow,
the frost and fog were your continual foes
and sunny Greece fresh freedom for your chest.

Part of my early days died when you died,
that literature of mercy from the dead

bequeathed to us at large. I can see
Wolfit clutching the curtains after *Lear*,
breathless, dramatic. But for real air

you struggled at the end. Each scene unrolled.
And Aberdeen, I think, was your age of gold
confident, incisive.
                                So we climb
breathlessly our hills, and one fine dawn
Apollo springs from Delphi in a blaze

that gilds each tombstone with eternal Greece.

The Wife Speaks

My head, she says, is sore,
he will not shift from bed.
Somewhere a marble door
is opening as I shed

the weighted clothes I wear,
the jacket of his will,
and soon, I think, I'll share
the random beautiful

flowers of the final field
and leave the sheets behind
wet to each weary fold
that imitates my mind.

For Champers

You died, mewing
with pain on the
vet's scrubbed table.

The icy Bible says
that an animal
has no soul,

your devoted gaze
empty, searching,
perpetually seeking

to cross the frontier.
Of flesh and fur
you were a slack lump

as we buried you
under a tree clump
in coal-black soil.

We stand in the wind
weeping, that the border
defeated us. A space

we watched for
is empty. A door
is forever shut

that you would push,
upright, with your paws,
almost human.

In the spring wind
you are lightly running
across the field

dappled with sunlight
or carrying a rabbit
floppily in your mouth.

29

Or you are curled
like a sleeping adder
on a red chair.

Champers, your name
is important.
            I proclaim
it openly to the wind

though in the black soil
you lie perpetually, innocent
one. Your fur will fade

into an enigma of bone,
a bare question.
And under the sun

I see you flying,
our miniature lion,
permanently alone.

Come, Fool

Come, fool, and tell me of your successes
just here where the wind combs the grasses
by this cemetery with its wooden crosses.

Come, gold-buttoned fool, with your new car
shining like a crab: walk over
this ancestral ground with its white flowers,

and talk in your loud voice of your gains,
your Midas jacket. Do you not feel the presence
of the empty-mouthed dead, and the dance

of the extinct girls.
                          Come, glassy fool,
stand by this stone and see your own name

excised as in your schooldays, an address
from your poor cottage to the universe

and then to your Mercedes and your hearse.

On the Grave an MA

In the scholarship of the grave
his tombstone has 'MA' on it.
As if a ghost might wear a glove
or a corpse might sport a bonnet,

and someone lying just there
who remembers a desk and school
and how one year he was a star
clever and most dutiful,

shining down on his own death,
the university of the grass.
Where after his painful breath
he saw himself serenely pass

in a black sparse and formal gown
above the skulls that lie below
and he hears the ghostly cheers resound
from that huge hall so long ago.

The Will

I must change my will.
I am not happy with the one
that I have written.

I should have left my money
to those whom I have wronged,
even the dead

who are standing at my bedside
with gaunt faces
and unforgiving eyes.

My breath
is like a train racing
towards an unimaginable station

where the stationmaster,
I think in sea blue,
has gold buttons.

But I am trembling
with the weight of my sins
though God is more than a lawyer

in a blue or grey day.
I am frightened.
Give me the pen.

Let me consider
a bequest to my father
whom I often disobeyed

and to that young girl
I once abandoned
in a ditch of sharp scent

and to my wife
who sits in a black chair
endlessly smiling

like a distraught doll.
The dead are really those
whom I wish to reward

for their vast patience
and for the wounds
I see in their eyes.

And above all
let what money I have
be for my comrades

who in far countries
or in red Flanders
died when young,

my imperfect comrades,
laughing and singing,
who opened beer bottles

in their new suits
working clothes, uniforms,
in fields of fresh grass.

The Death

In the old days we were nurses together.
Do you remember the Matron who used to lie in wait for us
when we returned from a dance.

Do you remember how we used to cycle in autumn
towards the hospital.

And the nights, the nights... I couldn't make my report
for tiredness.

In the morning the wards were fresh
with flowers and billowing curtains.
In the evening they were yellow with light
shining over the bloodstained bedclothes.

We were young and there was pain around us.
The old woman who told us she was pregnant,
the one who wished to pay her rent,
the one who waited eternally for her beau.

But we danced all night:
and left windows open for each other
and crawled through the shrubbery and trees.

It seems so long ago and we were young.
There was the patient who wrote a poem for me
and who was dying of TB.

And the surgeon with his cohort of nurses,
a whale trailed by small fish,
busy self-conscious prince,
who solved death by pomp.

Where are the matrons gone?

Some are religious now,
some sit in boarding houses,
some work for Oxfam,
some have outlived death.

And there was that night
when we returned from our taxi,
laughing and chattering.
We entered a night of stars,
its cherished jewellery,
and then the diminished light of the wards.

I'm sorry he died, that lad
who wrote the poem for you.

And the stars like innumerable eyes
regarded me.
Slowly, slowly, they went out
and the ward was a feral darkness
of horror and laughter.

Revenant

Dead, she swam towards me in the light.
'I have seen you before,' I said.
'I have sat on a chair beside you by the sea.'
Her tiny bones were like the tenderest flutes.
She smiled and smiled. I couldn't tell if it was
forgiveness or a waiting or a threat.
If there's a heaven it wasn't where those seats were.
If there's a hell, it's the absence, the return.

Many Years After

She glanced at me over her shoulder like a faun.
A girlish glance of forty years ago.
Her face was withered, and her eyes were dull.
There was a cute devilishness in her gaze.
My heart was almost broken as I saw
the short skirt whirl about her veined legs.
The sea is venomous and unmerciful.
I turned away. She would have seen my bald head
like a rock that's pestered by the salty tide.

Old Lady

The smiling old lady does not die
'O how happy we are to see you.
Keep up the good work,' say the visitors.

And the daughter smiles to herself
mourning the life that departs from her
day after day into the mirror.

'O you are a one,' say the visitors.
'Tough as they come.' And the daughter
blinks her red-rimmed eyes.

There is a bird that preys on her.
Smiling, it plucks out her heart
and eats it on the plate she's prepared.

From the Mad Ward

1

And as you wave goodbye
I know we shall not meet again
either here or earnestly
in another place beyond this pain.
I see your foxy face
disappear around a corner and
in perfect helplessness
raise my disappearing hand.

2

Dawn
The tree's inside
a nest of orange light
as if it were a brain
on fire with all the thoughts
that make it shake and burn –
you in your neat iron
infernal suit, going home
to the house where I once was
set in the green grass
but very distant now.

3

Come, take my hand,
be more authoritative. Understand
I am only a poor simple lunatic
come from the land of fruit into this brick
undernourished cage. And what I speak
has as little meaning as the creak
of a wooden door: or a bird's voice,
low, throaty, and anonymous.
I am of the world's refuse, scarecrow man
set to protect a decent field of corn
amid that autumn music. But my own
notes are a steady strawy monotone.

4

The lunatics are forking autumn leaves
into a barrow (such bare grizzly heads!).
The sky is cold and wintry and bright blue.
They work relentlessly but they speak no words,
the eternally deranged ones. Leaves at least may change
from green to gold and back to green again
but there's no change in their crew-cut hazy globes.
They're sweeping leaves away in the vast ward
of this great daylight and the clouds are still
portentous castles high above their heads.
For them there's only autumn and no spring.

5

The rain is falling. Poor Tom, poor Tom!
This is a dreadful landscape after the aplomb
of my early days. Come home to roost
are the fake alibis and the gross boast
settling on the wires. My dearest love,
wherever you are, cunning and piteous,
send me a picture I can look at, me
in your foxy eyes in miniature, now
reflected. Poor Tom, poor Tom!
Wind wanderer, rain sufferer, far from home!

The Old Lady

1

In the white house opposite me lives an old lady.
I am so lonely, she says, I am so dreadfully alone.

My husband is dead and my radio, blue as a cuckoo,
is what I depend on – I am frightened by the TV.

There you see his photograph on the wall. He was innocent as
    water.
In the Great War he was a naive sleep walker.

And consequently I sit here in my opaque nightgown.
And I read Ouspensky below the tranquil stars.

Time falls like rain, directly, oppressively, downwards.
It bubbles in the barrel at the corner of the house.

I am like one of the Brontës but without religion.
The rabbits in lithe rings play in front of my door,

in the field where the vacant cow chews dewy grass blades.
I seem to look through windows eternally at the sky.

I am frightened and I do not know what I am frightened of.
The sunsets which blaze in the evening are my theatre,

an old lady in rags of time listening to the radio
which is almost hidden in a nest and rag-bag of souvenirs.

You who sit at your desk, what do you think of,
as you gather the world into some sort of order,

which I cannot do, for I have no masterful story,
unless I compare myself with a witch at a poisoned well

in a house slightly off-centre, weird, distorted.
Tell me what time is, inscrutable scholar,

when silence oppresses me. Summer is worse than winter,
occupied as it is by the nostalgic wings of birds

and their songs which emerge from an early heat haze.
I shall die soon, the earth will open quickly

just like a book and its plot will overwhelm me.
Listen, the evenings are tremendous and empty

and my son is in England married to an invisible wife.
And the radio speaks and the yellow phone never hums.

Tell me I can survive in the emptiness
when the landscape stares back at me, when the nameless hills
    gaze.

Do not leave me, I will hold out my hands towards you.
Please tell me how orphans renew themselves,

how they can gather the world around them like a nightgown,
when the owl hoots, and sorrow afflicts the mind.

Tell me why my husband's photograph stands in that field
high among the green grass while the Germans are steadily firing

like time itself, like rain, and his astonished spectacles
have bullet holes on the day when he cannot return.

2
Time destroys me, please tell me why, my sweet author.
It is a recalcitrant substance like tar, like childhood treacle.

We wade through it as into an eerie desert.
It is like air turned sour, it is like clotting air,

as clouds are, which are like clots in the sky.
Time is an appalling fiction, which nevertheless

is an eating fact. O let me summon about me
the ancient royalties when I was married and young,

an instant temporary star, of smiles and dramas.
The audience stood outside the church by a decaying wall

and I threw them my joys, fragments and orts of my raptures,
as if they were beggars, I tell you there was no time then,

only landscapes and people, magic, spaces and ceremonies.
I was an excited waker in a house of visions,

a devout actor on a chessboard of shadows and change,
and there were bells and perfumes. The world conspired with me,

was mine, was mine. It was no stranger then,
but simple, real, an unthought considerate neighbour,

and never a mirror. A mirror was constant in rooms,
a frame for my face, beautiful and responsive.

Through what holes did time leak then so that now I sleep
with bells of the Black Death on my aged breastbone

grapes of it, foreign buboes, a tinkling mail.
Remember the dead, they intone, remember the dead,

and the grass stands up in front of me, blatant and green.

3
I have lost my cat. I do not know what has happened to him.
Has he been poisoned, hit by a car, has he deserted me?

Cats sometimes leave one, they are so mysterious,
they take up their occupation in new homes,

smiling, aloof. I hope he hasn't abandoned me.
I would rather he were dead, lying in a overgrown ditch,

pecked at by crows like machines in the early morning.
That would be better than crass ingratitude.

Listen, sweet author, have you ever looked at a space,
hoping it will be filled by a live being.

That is how I stand at the door in the starlight
looking out for my cat – sometimes there are snails on the steps,

shiny and black, thin long snakes, in the moonlight,
lapping at the dish of milk, under black aerials.

But the space isn't filled. My cat lies in the ditch
with buttercups growing from his head, his chest, his belly,

uncoffined and wild, reduced to intimate bones,
and the space does not fill, he does not enter it

he won't become a tenant of that finite space.
Do you think he has deserted me, do you, sweet author,

do you think he's lying on some other red sofa,
petted by a stranger, blinking at a foreign fire.

4
I love roses but the garden begins to oppress me.
I am frightened that the grass will ascend to my sill,

athletic and gluttonous. And then the roses have thorns
against which not even my gloves protect me.

Ambitious rose, I have lost all ambition.
I sit on my green bench in the evening

and feel myself devoured by the trees, the hedges, the clouds,
while a self-confident buzzard sits on the fence post.

Is this an intimation of death, the exquisite hunger
of the grass for me, the sustained gaze of the sky,

the way in which the world becomes a mirror
in which I see only myself, murderous stain,

in a gown of patched green, interrupted by the cries
of birds, cockerels, seagulls, and trains.

Once I used to run about in the wood without fear,
now the world has invaded me, I am like a painting

45

in a fragrance of stupefaction. Soon I shan't see
my own husband's photograph, it will be devoured

by the mountains, the hills, the rivers, the roses and ferns.

5
Sweet author, tell me about your characters.
Sometimes at night I hear a knock at the door

but there's nothing there but the wind or a red cloud.
I am sick of books. I feel time pass by

bearing me with it on an unintelligible journey.
Sometimes I talk to the Jehovah's Witnesses

when they stand with their bibles at the door.
Who was it who betrayed Judas? I ask them.

I know Christ was betrayed but who betrayed Judas?
And why was Peter crucified upside down?

And were you ever, I ask, in the Garden of Gethsemane?
They are always well dressed in undiminished blue.

And then I have read about the Bahai and Hinduism.
And even Mohammedanism I have studied too.

Under what fragrant trees did the prophets
encounter God, and the absolute sky

harden from the provisional. Sweet author,
I want you to tell me these things,

sitting at your bare desk in the morning
when the wren is singing sweetly from a bush

and the young ones walk past, playing their radios,
and the red tractor is a red jewel in the field,

and my hands lie on my lap as in a painting
and the bushes are like clouds of smoke among the trees.

6

Do seagulls drink milk? I think it is the seagulls
who come down in the evening on their gluttonous wings

and drink the milk I put out for the cats.
They are the wild entries in my diaries

flown in from the large sea, sour and salty.
Their beaks are bigger than I remember.

Do they attack, I wonder, the tiny rabbits.
They have such cold eyes, with the blankness of scythes.

The stubble is brittle and bare. The world is a picture
signed by no author. Why should I switch a spade

from one place to another on my lawn?
Wild thing, descend from heaven. We suffer

the scrutiny of the wren, the berries' instancy.
Seagulls were never ashen. They eat no pictures,

but herring and mackerel. If they should drink milk!
If they should be tamed, imperious voyeurs,

if they should eat bread,
if they should perch on a cloudy branch.

In Glasgow

As in the taxi cab
we turned up Alexandra Parade
the name returned to me
in the voice of my dead
otherwise country-bred
mother.

And suddenly I saw her
trim as a maid
walking beside
the bible-black cab,
in a flowery dress
of white and blue,
happy, intent.
And the way she went
was innocent too,
as if she would say,
How can you ride
while I'm walking beside
you on the street.

But before I could say,
Please take a seat
on this iron cold day
you'd disappeared
into a cloud
which suddenly towered
over your Glasgow,
warm and adored,

as if somewhere you'd slipped
quick and abrupt
through a tenement close

and the cab sped on
into the new
concrete Glasgow

and out of the dream
I stepped quite alone

into Easterhouse,
draughty, anonymous,
collection of stone.

Nurses

Nurses, you look so young and cheerful
among these coughing wheezing shouting old men.
You remind us of the possibilities of joy,
of births and marriages and christenings.
To be so elegant in all that pain,
to be so eloquent in all that blood.
Be beautiful, bright-haired, and do not cry.
Think of your powder, combs and lipsticks.
Place your pink mirrors in the midst of death.
No, it's not irreverent to choose
shoes or such a belt or such a ribbon.
Let old men feast on you with their gluttonous eyes.
This is where loveliness is tested
at the edge of things, where even a knife's glitter
reflected in a watch your boyfriend gave you
speaks of a morning without monument
or heavy statues which the wind can move.

The Stranger

Once being ill you woke at 4 a.m.
and sat on the chair in the living-room.
A stranger came in and sat opposite.

All night you talked to him about your life,
its paucities, complaints, and pauperdom.
He sat and listened, never speaking a word.

At dawn he rose, and walked away from you.
The red sun was streaking the old chair.
You did not hear the door open or shut.

It was quite strange, really it was quite strange,
his silence and his patience, and your words
going on and on in the quietness of your house.

Students

To the end of our lives, students,
who thought once students wore gowns
and took notes in the light of large windows –

but students still till our deaths
haggardly studying leaves
and trying to locate the professor

whose words would be the last Amen.
Not easy in tangled streets to find
MAs with stone folios.

However, students we remain
and take with us our pens
to note as we turn on our pillow

the first answer moving into shadow,

the pen writing more rapidly
in harmony with our breath towards morning.

The Old Poet

Before I go over the horizon of the dark
let me do my last poetry reading in a hall
where there are no excuses from the chairman,
and the room is full of fragrance. And people cry
to think of their bones shining towards evening.
And the hall is crammed with leafy presences,
the dead, the living, and all who were friends to me
when I grew up in the hot mists of June.
And like Eurydice I'll say farewell to them
as I'm gathered to the shades in the lyre's sound
and the steps climb steadily towards a daylight
which I shall never see as my wings fold.

Sometimes I Remember

Sometimes I remember the poor relations
in these huge Russian novels, at the edge of
the loud action, with their threadbare gloves
endlessly sitting in rooms while the spurred counts
stride quickly in and out. Poor relations,
no one listens to you, your voices are so faint,
no one can hear you, and you sit there
in the hollow quietness like aspidistras
in their Victorian bowls. Elsewhere,
there is the noise of gunnery, oaths,
men parting tearfully with silver watches,
medallions, in the wind. The horses gulping
for air, pure air. The big book expanding
from fields where a whole class died. No,
no one listens to you. They rush out shouting
pointing at the smoke, and as you wait
white carved ceilings fall and pictures melt,
countesses are rushing through the fire
parasols over their heads.

For Livingstone, the Explorer

Explorer of dark forest,
intrepid moralist,
hater of the slave trade,
forsaker of your family.

Exploration was your hair shirt,
your joy was the sunset
and the sunrise of Africa,
its stupendous muddy star.

Onward you travelled
through sharp and wild
forest, stone mirrors.
There were few chairs,

comfortable tables.
On the contrary horses
expiring in ditches.
You heard snatches

of dialect: God's word.
Harrowed
by dysentery, boils,
pagan rituals

the skulls of slaves,
the leaky sieves
of captainless boats,
razor-sharp reeds.

The will, the will!
This would prevail,
diamond-hard,
though the hand were scarred,

till the body flagged.
Finally fatigued,
a rickle of bones,
you watched the aged lions

encircling you.
Wife's bones refined
elsewhere: son
hard to contain.

In the forest you lay,
imperishable, gray,
a moral diamond,
a will designed

to weather fierce thorns.
To stand by huge lakes
improvident as mirrors,
generous windless

these foreign waters,
your reflection adorns.

2

London

In St James Park, the ducks
are swimming in the river, beside which
the deck chairs sit untenanted. The
policemen stroll among the bluish mist
rustling the leaves. Along the Mall
alternate lamp posts wear high crowns.
The gates of Buckingham Palace
are locked. At Horse Guards Parade
the riders sit on their seven black horses
one of which pees copiously. The helmets
are drawn low on the faces, in a beaten
lowering gold.
             In Soho the girls strip
to bushes and bare bottoms, their eyes
expressionless as pebbles, smiling a little
into the large mirrors, where the red
sofas are reflected.
                The guide
in the House of Commons says, 'It's
all tradition. Don't sit on the seats.'
The bad big paintings show
Charles beheaded, Nelson in his triumph.
In the cold Great Hall, tennis balls were found
used by Henry the Eighth and his ladies.
In Soho,
blue films go on all night. Remember
the flesh is not traditional, like the ceilings
of the two Parliaments. The great legs
slowly open. The body arches backward.
Over the bridge the hair of the dead head sprays.

Turkey

1

Flagged, it sets out, the tourist fleet,
for Rhodes or Cos.
The sun nets its sides,
as once we know they searched for the Golden Fleece.
Inflation soars, for the poor a harsh ladder
among the fictitious coloured sails.

2

A shining moon.
     The moon that brings them home
to their familiar beloved Turkey,
their frugal villages.
       Elsewhere, Istanbul
profuse and threatening. The golden bird,
a cockerel surely, brutally bespurred,
outlasts these crops: outlasts Byzantium.

3

Byzantine dream on the edge of things!
They brought down Venice when their armies seized it,
impelled Columbus to America.

America, magnet of our wanderings,
its jewelled armoury and its pointed missiles
a landlord subsidising bracelets, rings.

4

America, that golden heathendom.
This century's flamboyant campfire
to which we steer on our new bicycles.

Dramatic Hollywood above our dust,
more colourful than carpet. Let us float
towards it, its fertile fabulous breasts.

5
Dung, manure. Stopped toilets. So
we all squat in our humanity,
from which there is a stink among roses.
    Art is what
we raise to befriend us, brighter than a mirror,
to alter that abiding torrid smell,
to dye the subjective and immediate.

6
The sky is blazing blue.
                    Not angels pass
with European wings of purest white,
but ghosts of goats feeding from cloud to cloud
for perhaps a year or more.
                    And water too
bubbling freshly in that seamless blue.

7
An old woman weighed down with wood
passes along the road as in Lewis.
If she should stop, overwhelmed by the grass
her grave should be just there, freshly scented,
paltry and obscure, as evening swells
opulently above her, cheaply painted.

8
Profound meaning. Countries have their flags
and yet beyond them are the same needs.
Let us proclaim them unreasoning rags
hung above our common farms and graveyards.

If it were not for that provincial moon,
our close familiar, pendent by that fence,
large-breasted mother, passive and divine,
convincing globe of local affluence.

9

An old woman leans against the jewellery shop.
Behind her the small blue Visa-
shape of our ecstatic moveable heaven.

10

The one road points towards the west,
charismatic, technical.
                    To be impelled
past the warm moon of secretive Diana.

Let not the music of the phenomena
be played on an instrument of instant keys.

11

How can the heart be cosmopolitan,
in wasteful commonness.
            Prudence spares
an avenue or lane for itself.

This hot sun is like a wolf
licking its chops.
            Northernness has
mirrors and the foliage of frost.

12

Mirrors, ice, extravagances of snow.
Absences which need books like flowers.
Avid complexities of theatres,
enigmas, and interiors and furs.
Enchanted labyrinths.
            (And fresh Aprils
shadowy regimes of the chaffinch.
At-homes of nature in its temperate
seasonal restructurings of wind and cloud.)

13
Peace to all others.
              But geology
particular is mine. Provincial sky.
Haphazard and particular treasury.
Gravestones, nurseries. Fidelity
to moons and stones.
The curious parlance of heredity.
The echoes and the chains.
Miniature portraits of a beloved land.

Malta

The Mediterranean froths at the rocks just as at home
except that the Phoenicians were here once, and the Romans,
and Neptune once accepted the fragments of planes.

How opposite they are, Lewis and the Mediterranean,
the rigid stony church and these Virgin Maries
fixed in a heaven of brilliant blue.

How shall I love this incense, these opulent pictures,
these altars, tombs, these flaking meagre Christs,
these stories of miraculous cures, and instant saints.

And yet the rocks are like home, and the sea is familiar,
but the gods, the gods, what shall I say of you,
as you recline in water in this astounding sun.

You open your arms to those who love Apollo,
who plunge from rocks into your warm brine
you lavish your gifts on those who do not know the North.

But the glacial North has its own stories,
its wolves and ice, its bleak fanaticisms,
its poets who sing of freezing headlands,

and for whom there is no immortality. Drownings
are real drownings: and the gods do not rescue,
as singing dolphins might, those who cannot breathe,

nor does the Virgin hold out her saving arms.

See, I walk among souvenirs, Roman heads,
the stony statues of senators, the Phoenician boats,
knights who stare out at me from bluish mail.

And I cast my shadow over these red flowers
where they grow toughly out of a foreign geology,
and the goddess who smells of milk and belongs to the earth.

I belong to the ice and the stories of ghosts
and the snow which colours unechoing houses
and the eagles which descend over the white hill.

These dry walls have many resonances
and the lyres of gods and the secrets of romance
and incestuous possession and the poverty of clothes

hanging from tenement windows among bricks
far from the transparent marble of the gods
and their jewelled chairs and their bones of crystal.

Nevertheless I must return to my icy theorems,
to the tempestuous thunders, to my nostalgic autumns,
where the leaves turn yellow and my nostrils feel the cold,

to my furs and clouds, to the children in their uniforms,
to my woods and foliage, to the sudden lightnings,
to the transparences of October, to the Christmas snows.

So farewell to the gods, to their liquid presences,
farewell to the statues formed in impermanent gilt,
to the rocks without mussels, to the acres without grass,

to the hot afternoons which burn even the Virgin Maries,
to the processions that are colourful with their portable statues,
and to the clear moon that turns us happily towards home.

On the Golan Heights

On the Golan Heights there are unexploded mines,
and the sweet red flowers grow around them.
The electronic fence will betray the nose of a dog.

Something is waiting for us in history like an unexploded mine
though we sweep the sky like radar.
It is waiting for us,
this terrible destiny.

It is in the stones and among the flowers,
it is in the clouds, in the grass,
it is like a safe waiting to be opened,

our destiny, dreadful and inevitable.
Our fate dressed in black crossing the golden field
when the mine like a bouquet explodes.

London

The leaves are blowing about the streets of London.
In the second-hand bookshops bearded men are peering through
    magnifying glasses.
In Soho the naked girl bends over and peers through her bush of
    hair.

The planes rise over Gatwick and Heathrow.
At Earl's Court a busker is playing a guitar.
In a publisher's office an editor stubs out another cigarette.

And the leaves are blowing about the fruit and flower stalls
in the blue mist of autumn, in the complex strata of autumn,
and the smell of apples in a memory of absence here as anywhere
    else.

Aberdeen

Sparkling leaves... I remember Aberdeen,
my university days. Oil's brimming now
where once I used to study Gaelic, Latin,
in Duthie Park with pale and lowered brow.

Shall oil restore us? Virgil's Hades glooms
with fictional ghosts, implacable and proud.
From the North Sea the goggled diver looms.
On Summer St, pop lyrics, clear and loud,

troubled the leaves and me while the green trams
skid down their wires. Riches, they say, now pour
from waters Arctic-cold: and Babychams
remind Americans of the wells they bore

far from their stores and states. Shall Virgil live,
and in that granite cage Lucretius
despise religion, say we must forgive
each other on a planet spinning loose

among pure leaves of ice. I have my wells
deeper than these, and see on Union St
the coupled virginal hilarious girls
with their cracked Woolworth handbags laugh and greet

the pimply boys, brylcreemed and unheroic
oiled with their sex. Riches are what we find
in what is transient, perilous, and oblique,
the random glitter of the sun and wind,

the helmets of the sunrise: and our oil
that constant energy that feeds our loves
while ghosts in lumbering suits rise from their toil
and the furious vigour of fermenting graves.

Silver

It was in the market that I saw the sparkle of silver
even among the books, the videos, the radios and the fruit.

It was there that I saw the thin river of silver
though there were children's toys, rings, cufflinks, and rugs.

It was there in spite of the beautiful lady at one of the stalls
who had long black hair streaming down her shoulders

that I saw the meagre illumination of silver like fish
and heard the gluttonous cry of the customer

and saw the raven's shadow fall over the market, and the vulture's:
while the cat scurried away into the shade of a tree

and all that was beautiful and colourful was turned to silver
on a calm cool day in Valetta under a blue sky.

3

The Well

The children are haunted by the well.
They brim the bucket with pure water,
and pour it over the tilted rim
in a wasteful avalanche of laughter.

There is a well in my mind's eye
we visited with our two pails,
in summer's brilliant brief glory.
Its eye was large and round and chill.

The children jump with happy glee.
This is our story: gravity pulls
us closer to the grassy ground.
But in our youth delighted bubbles

rise in us without a reason.
We are so wasteful of our days.
The serene eye will keep its season
reflecting variously what is.

And so too after our hands cease
to pull the bucket from the well
in our tiny local sparkling place
as if it might be universal.

The Song

In the song someone is crying.
Outside there is frost and snow.
The frost stares back at us with tearless face.
But in the song someone is crying
because of the mortality of man,
because he carries his grave with him
to the safety of grass.
Beauty is so fine and terrible.
It makes our hands shake, our eyes wet.
Outside the window there is frost and snow.
Beauty consistently breaks the heart.
The beautiful are like vases, as Keats said.
Their stories are so fine, so terrible.
The beautiful ones touch us so grievously.
'The still unravished brides.'

I Remember

I remember that castle
standing on the hill
and the sea misty with heat.
It all seems quite recent
and yet it is more than thirty years
since I first saw them.

Nothing remains the same
though they remain the same.
Though my heart stirs
I cannot now see them
as young as I saw them
in that lovely summer,

which I thought eternal.
There was a brilliant sparkle.
There were white sails.
A queenly liner
divided the water
in that prodigious dance.

If it were not so
I would have told you.
Heaven was there
with the exact shadows
of boats and liners
and legendary islands.

My eyes fade.
Habit that protects us
is now protecting me
from that fertile dazzle,
the hot cage
of that empty castle.

Absolutely to fear
that tremendous joy,
that excessive excitement!
That absolute fire
to turn away from
into my small room,

compulsively tidy
with its chosen forms,
its remembered phantoms,
that smell of sharp brine,
and the tall shadows
of many who are dead.

The heart almost breaks
not again to feel it,
that early vigorous fire,
and the water dancing
around that white liner
setting off for somewhere else.

Teachers

I have met old teachers in strange places.
Some have had strokes, some play the violin
in a quiet little heaven of their own.
And some are standing on the banks of Hades
with books about Julius Caesar in their hands,
English grammar, absolute ablative.
Sometimes a huge wind blows them away,
the leaves of autumn. Sometimes in the snow
wearing their gowns of chalk they are writing.
I have met the old teachers in strange places
and there are apples trembling in their hands.

Aberdeen

In that cage of granite
I used to shout out lines from *Othello*
as I passed the cemeteries.

Put up your bright swords or the dew will rust them.

And the swords were put up in the air
mistakenly
instead of back in their scabbards,
graves for their rays.

Putting out the Ashes

A night such as we have never known,
millions of stars, shooting stars, a moon.
I stand and breathe the sky. It is breathing.
The supernatural light rests on the bin

freezing it to a palpable brilliant vase
from Greece perhaps, though it is packed with waste.
This is a marvellous spendthrift universe
a poet throwing off verse after verse.

Christmas Tree

The Christmas tree shines over the graves.
Silent colourful bells, your colourful chime
is not a natural wintry paradigm.

Velvety globes, baroquely harvested,
you seem to flourish over the bones
in a delightful sweet insouciance.

Artistic berries, opulent orbs,
frosty branches, tiny azure crowns,
you rise above the urbs of skeletons.

Lit too remarkably by the imagination,
a brilliant unrooted constellation
shining over our cold habitual stones.

Santa Claus

Just like a god you bring your unearned presents.
How across wastes of ice, young ears have listened

to your inaudible journey towards their house.
Red-robed you are and rich and gorgeous

and never again will the night appear the same.
Out of your limitless emporium

you bring your gifts (perhaps unmerited).
Justice is different from this plenitude

which they must learn by meagreness to forget
when, later on, the enviable bracelet

will tighten round their wrists or melt like dew,
as they will know. There's no free rendezvous.

Hallowe'en

This small child has an old man's face,
an old man's clayey bleak unquestioning face.
He plays the violin and sings a song,
small, expressionless, unquestioning.

And then after he has played he pulls
the mask away, and there he stands
fresh-faced and laughing with blonde curls
and from the grave extends his hands.

Macbeth and the Witches

When the sun was white and wintry and drained of energy
Macbeth met the witches under the rim of the sky.
Why did you confirm my evil, he said.

And the witches who were lighting thorns in the cold winter said,
There is a play that one plays when the summer is over
and you happened to be one of the cards in our hand,

a deformed king with a coat too large for him
and a crown that sizzled in the white wintry sky.
These things are after all not important

except to those who suffer, who are not important.
Feeling belongs to the spring and the ignorance of lovers.
Here in this wood it is a question of passing the time,

and the abstract intellect constructs dramas
with a queen and a pawn and the immortal joker
who faces two ways at the frosty January gates.

Let be, let be, it was quite a nice structure.
And truth after all can be played with under the sun
which is fading slowly towards a renaissance of leaves.

Come, join us, join us, at the unimportant edge of things
wearing your coat of blood with the hole in the breast.
This is the west. The east has innocent wings.

The Cuckoo

Today you heard the cuckoo for the first time
this year. It seems important to you,
this voice from the grave of clouds.

Listen, it speaks to you at least thrice,
once for living and once for death
and once for what is beyond death,
the coming alive again out of the gorse.

The Fence

Children running and playing
outside the school
your energy is beautiful.

What bows us down
is the invisible fence
at which we buck
then subside to a slow walk

dignified, honourable,
the wiry ethics
that we have created
in the middle of the fresh air.

The Spider

The spider's at the centre of the web
on this fine autumn day.
There he is clinging to our window pane.
Yesterday he crawled like an astronaut
breeding a line behind him,
or like a crab swaying through air not water.
He is not catching any flies.
He lives on air as poets do
and the justice of heaven.
The day is perfectly still,
a technique without ideas
as his web is,
a structure with nothing in it but itself.
To the quiet woods the cones are falling
and the trees are still on the hill.
What are you, spider, who are you
hunched brown and terrible
at the centre of your strands.
So much has been truly made,
the great responsible dead,
autumn so clean and pure,
and the fat spider
at his lean scant trade.

Early Spring

The crocuses are out in January
in their green and purple
and I have seen the gorse as well.
The seasons do not know themselves,
they are delirious with promise.
They stay awake with excitement instead of sleeping
as I did in my first job
when I was bringing learning to the young.
See, even the clouds are a different colour
they too are purple
they too have this early freshness.

Last night I was reading of an old man
who scouring among graves would find coffin wood
from which he would make violins.

Welcome

The sun is flashing from the hot gate.
Stranger, do not fear to come in.
There is cool water in the basin,
and there are shadows in the small rooms.
Remove your tunic and show yourself
entirely as the Muse,
who walks the dusty road in the summer.
         Please excuse
the tiles which are not marble,
the absence of statues from the hall.
But in the very depths of the hot garden
you will find an ordinary cool well.

The Gaelic Proverb

The Gaelic proverb says,
sad is the state of the house
without a child or cat.

But sad is the state of the child
who carries his house on his back
like a trapped snail.

And the cat who cannot go out
into the deep greenery
but sits on the spinster's lap,
narrow and infertile,
as the wild sun goes down.

You

You come towards me
through the haze of summer
under the trembling of the airy leaves.

You are carrying a bag,
you look old and shrunken,
you seem like a lost tourist.

Where have you come from?
Out of the land of death
with its million ghosts,
carbon copies of the real.

Forgive me, forgive me, I cry.
I didn't talk to you
as much as I should have done.

I was on my exhausting ladder
climbing towards the ideal poem
and my time was limited.

I didn't talk to you
about the events of your local day.

Now you come towards me
walking very heavily
and sometimes stopping to rest

as I do too
more and more
on this impossible journey

of continual papers
which blow like leaves
down an infernal hole.

And the day is hazy
with the sleep of summer
and you sit down on a bench
wiping your brow

and staring down at your shoes
which are scuffed with dust
as if they were a mirror
of those remembered nights

of silence and of exile

of the difference between two lives.

Aunt

Good luck to you

as you set off to college,
let the weight of civilisation be not too heavy on your shoulders

as you carry your small nephew

laughingly like a horse
and he pulls at your face

which is a map of impermanent skin.

Shakespeare

The buzzard's shadow flies across the grass.
I hear the tiny and industrious mouse.

King and peasant...
                          I toil at this white page.
Shakespeare passes, large and perilous.

My pen is a small beak, nibbling, nervous.
Acres are swallowed by that confident shade.

Escape

I ran away from the Home, he said.
They tried to tug me from the gate
I'd anchored myself to. I wanted home
to be among the wind and light.

No, I cried, no. No, no,
I do not want to be with the dead
staring dully out at the spring.
I feel light heels on my old feet.

I hung on to the knotted wood
which humbly outlasts us by good grace.
The ground was glinting turbulent mud,
the seagulls wild and precious.

They set me in a wheelchair and
I found a way of stopping them.
I stuck my fingers in the rays
to halt it in a pulsing flame

as the white ones tugged me from the sky
and the red eye that ruled the field
where the lumpy muddy pillows die
to the airy barley's wavy yield.

The Theft of the Vases

The lion-headed vases have disappeared.
Someone has stolen them and has left no trace.
(Pity I'm no detective, just a bard.)

The wall looks bare without them. Newly-painted
they'll be in England (Europe) now perhaps.
Criminals have sharp and clever maps.

What can I say? Eternity, he said,
gravely rotates about the Grecian urn,
a glamorous fixture high above the dead.

So these exist though they are somewhere else,
and there are spaces where they used to be.
Eternity exists in another place,

and in some alien unknown garden
our two eternal vases turn and turn.

Two Pieces

1

The girl is dancing the sword dance.
The piper who is fat and who wears a big red kilt and a wide black
      belt
is playing, while tapping his feet on the floor.
The girl is dancing on the perimeter of the two crossed swords.
Now the music accelerates and her feet also accelerate.
She dances in and out of the quadrants made by the swords.
She is intent on the swords.
The music becomes faster and faster as do the movements of the
      girl who is dancing on tiptoe.
The swords, the swords, can she avoid the swords, the dark-haired
      girl with the green kilt, the velvet black silver-buttoned
      jacket, the strong yet delicate legs.
Can she avoid the playful ferocity of the swords?
Suddenly the music stops, she stops simultaneously, her hands
      on her hips,
she bows to the audience and runs over to her mother bearing the
      two swords
with the cheap jewels in them.

2

A large fat man is throwing the caber.
A lame boy is trying to climb the slippery pole.
The tents are selling sweets and balloons.
A boy wearing a blue kilt, a blue jacket, a blue cap with a feather in it
and blue stockings, is dancing on the small wooden stage.
The girls and boys in the two-legged race stumble and fall
      laughing on the grass.
The lame boy is still climbing, gripping the pole like a monkey,
      his teeth clenched.
Outside one tent are empty beer cans. A man is shooting at clay
      pigeons against a blue sky.
The piper has been playing in the same spot for two hours.
A little girl is crying while stretching her hands out to an airy red
      balloon,
which floats over the field,
over the fat men who are toiling at the caber,
and the pale determined boy who is still trying to climb the
      slippery pole.

Stones

Stones, I stand here like a conductor.
You are my orchestra of the quotidian.

I make a thistle rise among you.
It has fine and purple crowns.

I attribute royalty to you,
who are a determined proletarian.

I introduce you to the stars
some of which are smoking extinct stones.

I say 'Triumph' to you.
You will rise from your whispers and be royalty.

You will be a court of new princes
and colours like courtiers will walk among you
in their yellows and reds.

You will aggrandise the horizon,
stones that are the lords of every day.

On a Clear Day

On a clear day one can see one's childhood
with comics one worshipped and the cigarette cards
with all the colourful flowers on them
and those whose mouths have been closed by salt
jumping up and down in their yellow strips.

It is clear and causeless, and the old fat lady
whom we all laughed at is carrying her errands
towards her thatched house; and the lark
is winding upwards into the blue sky
above its nest with the secret speckled eggs.

Nothing is changing, and the bearded men
are sitting in the sun: and the scythe
flashes among the corn: and on the moorland
the owl is glaring with insomniac eyes:

and there is no wind anywhere at all.

Waiting for the Ferry

Waiting for the ferry I see cans, bottles, and stones,
cartons, papers, rags, ropes and old tyres.
The ferry is crossing and recrossing the dirty river.
Afloat in the water are fag ends, orange rinds.

No angels here, only repetitiveness.
An old lady with a stick is patiently waiting to cross.
From the ferry I can hear a raucous music.

I imagine in the river a dead horse

whose head is made of uranium, or iron,
with moss about the eyes which are bottle-green,
and its mane twisted and tough like old wire.

Let me step on the shore, it cries, let me be seen
by admirers among buttercups swishing my tail
which is a flurry of frayed ropes and rainbow oil.

A Story

The taxi driver and the madman fought
at two in the morning in a Glasgow 'scheme',
one with a sword and one with a rusty rail.

'Never will I pay you,' the madman shouted,
'I would rather kill you with this pure weapon.
Defend yourself, my harsh exploitative foe.'

And the moonlight shone on them and on the new Glasgow
and the rusty rail fenced against the sword
and it was a lovely lyrical night, all yellow.

And the cab driver pushed the madman back.
'I've got you now,' he said, with a rusty thrust,
and the swordsman fell in an arc across the moon.

And the cabman said, 'Enough, I'll leave your money,
outrageous madman, for this is a mad night
of gold and silver, so farewell,' and laughed

and drove away towards the golden city
from the pure sword, so dangerous and bare,
and washed the rust away from his yellow hand.

The Poet

Chained at his desk
like Prometheus
the vulture eats him:

dressed in its black tails
its breath furious and sour,
it's like a clock that never fails:

in its smart evening dress it towers
out of the sunset's ravening pictures.

No Muses

No, it's not a question of waiting for a voice from the sky
as in ancient days,

or sitting at a desk like Vergil while the empire prospered around
him.

There is no such voice, objective and distant and impartial,
there are no Muses dressed in imperial blue.

It is more likely to be a flash from a piece of glass or from an old
mirror,
it is more likely to be a squint-eyed man handing out crooked
rifles at a fair,
it is more likely to be a girl swaying past in durable denims.

Vergil perfecting his lines in the seclusion of an eclogue
writing with a bronze pen about the golden outspread eagle,
did you believe in the gods, in Elysium and in Hades?

For myself I have looked out of a train window
and seen a pheasant dressed in the tranquillity of stained glass
and I have heard an Ulsterman praising a blue church
set in a landscape of perishing rich green
and he was fat and loud-mouthed and he said, All Catholics are
ugly,
and I have seen a child gazing into a well
beside a red gnome on an autumn morning.

And I have seen a wizened old woman standing greyly by a
flourishing rose,

and a cat with emerald eyes stalking a robin:

and there is no calm glaze of an empire where I live
or praise for a bloodstained army fording a river
and seeing their red reflections in the water
and their pikes stuck up like a forest of branches
while the women squeal like rabbits in the undergrowth.

And a cool imperator sips from a glass of cold wine.

No, there is only the random kaleidoscope of images,
our wheel which knows no gods and is ignorant of fortune
and it is there that on a good day I labour

while the peasant bowed under his load trudges along a road
that does not lead particularly anywhere though the sun is hot on
    his shoulder.

At a Poetry Reading

After I'd recited my poems in Folkestone
you came to speak to me.
You were from Lewis.

The rich solid stone houses stand by the sea shore.
The sea sparkles.

Near Dover they're digging the Channel Tunnel
through miles of water.
At night there are avenues of light.

During the war shells from Calais travelled
towards this land of stockbrokers.

The sea is perhaps the same around Lewis and here.
It is a salt ring of blue.

The Arts Centre speaks of Brecht, Pinter, Shaw.
There are abstract paintings on the walls.

My island, you are a distant diamond in my consciousness.
Women with little dogs walk this esplanade.

England is another country, richer than us.
We belong to the sparse climate of peasants.

The land becomes dearer, pricier, as the lorries accelerate from
      Europe,
the houses become golden.

And we are far in the north, our dearness is different,
an affair of thistles.

This is where the future is. It has not known our language.
I think however it's possible

that some of our villagers might have been drowned here,
defending the white cliffs made of chalk.

We are scattered to the wind, even towards riches
And all that unites us is the sea,

resonant, indifferent, estranging,
where Arnold for a moment forgot his chalk
and pierced the heart with absence.

Compulsory Retirement

Soon I shall be summarily summoned
by specious story to the professor's
prosaic study, where I shall be told
that my profound poetry of the desolate ditches
is not fashionable: that unserious scholars
no longer demand it: it is difficult.
Armed Angles do not attract them
nor Saxon swords naked against Norsemen
decorate dreams with turbulent thorns.
Nor does the whaleway widowing wan wives
with wave's random glintings, reverberate.
Nor do the shrieking sea gulls, blunt-beaked,
fly in familiar air, forsaking
denuded northern nests. Nor the cuckoo's
call from tall trees in ambiguous April
enchant them, inelegant in dour denims,
or haunted hall absent of accolade
and crested chief tremendously torment them,
precarious pilgrims with sustaining staffs
in the wind's cross-referenced whining wail.
Unsurrendering mail at wall and water
does not stand up straight in their sight,
as someone says, 'Arms will not abate
nor will weaken' as across quiet quad
in leaf storms, in azure autumn air,
lovers proliferate in the poetic season
of learning's lambent and leaf-fringed courts.
Not on stony lingo such as yours
do their thoughts linger, but of May's music
preferring to partake they in scarves
trail across the transient, adore
the pleasing present. And so sign here
my salutary surrender unheroic
in oblique offices, though open arms
enclasp me emptily. Wife is widowed
of all but spare pension. Brilliant-beaked
she swoops superbly on you, sweetness lost
in summer's scent, now severely soured,
by failure's faltering footsteps, in a room

where you'll reside till bright and assiduous April
cause ache in heart, and cuckoo calls clearly
from briny waters, melancholy miles
and furious feathered migrant she departs.

Milton

Out of the immense darkness your voice rose.
It was a fertile spring which defied
the excised stone, and the destruction of your hopes.
It wasn't the will, will cannot construct music,
which rises in solid pillar upon pillar,
to a new temple which was not built by hands.
You hear the louts and hooligans in the night
in their vanishing velvets and cold arrogance,
the wine guzzlers who splash blood on the wall,
those who have escaped the iron individualism of your planet –
yet the music will not cease in the moving darkness,
it creates Adam and Eve in their tremulousness,
it creates the devil elegant in snakelike green,
it creates a blitz of angels falling from the sky.
In spite of the destruction of hope, the music . . .
In your hebraic cloth, the holiness of your inspiration,
your head is an astronomy of stars, your ardour is relentless,
the music defies the darkness, and is heroic,
it renews itself endlessly in the reclusive silence of art.

Who cannot take comfort from you, old rancorous one
for whom the exact notation of nature was not enough,
for whom there were no real elegies even of the drowned?
You sing out of your blindness like a beggar,
at the extinct silence of your hopes you will not be silenced,
the holy doves perch on your scholarly shoulders
and common humanity is forgiven by your spartan star.
Your hearse is constructed of music
and your poems are as lasting as the towers of London,
its palaces and castles.
It is the bright architecture that soars out of the dark,
marvellous blind rancorous one who submitted your theology to
    death
and who are resurrected over and over in your music,
putting off the leaves, learning a classical bareness,
the handsome Apollo who wished to know all the rays of the sun
but who bumps in the end against the pillars of his own verse.

The Scholar

The bitter scholar remembers how his monographs
disappeared down a chute in the middle of his days,
how he stuttered at the interview when questioned about admin.,
how his rivals pounced on his fresh book and munched it.
The sky darkened steadily since his undergraduate years
when he sparkled like a diamond at the café table
outside which there was an orchard with ripening apple trees.
Was it his life that infected his studies
and drew his energies away from his papers.
Was it his shyness that made him fall silent
among the coteries in the Dining Hall.
Was it that everything had already been written about his
        favourite author.
Did he not know seamanship well enough to understand Conrad.
Then he withdrew. And the apple-bottomed students
were moving eagerly towards fresher voices
which combined witticisms with transatlantic power.
Who could be said betrayed him? Some sinuous Judas
hiding among the trees, among the blossoms.
Let him remember his early days before his office was denuded,
before the scholars ceased to consult him,
before timidity overwhelmed him in the eternal silence,
when literature used to reflect his youthful optimism
and the leaves of the trees were the leaves of precious poems
before literature itself, allied to power and place,
became the plaything of men agile with word processors,
before idealism drained away from his heart
on a battleground which he had never thought existed
in a world which he loved once in that early café
whose owner could talk knowledgeably about Proust.

The Scholar Says Goodbye

Goodbye Gray, also gaunt Gourlay,
long-legged swooping Lily (Ms) goodbye,
and many others of the curious cruxes,
who in warm nest numerously wrought
unprofitable papers. Fond farewell
to copious coffees in the Common Room,
deliberate discussions, while the *Times*
sheets lay scattered on the tea-wet table.
A fond farewell
to the sharp plebeian powerful secretary,
abrupt and acid. O a fond farewell
to leisured lawns, basking under bells
in summer when the students sprawled slackly
in shining white blouses, bonny books
held in faintly shadowed freckly hands.
A fond farewell to the carved coat of arms
with the minatory motto. Also to
library and lectern, spire and scroll,
leather armchairs and the *Listener*,
to these I say farewell and the cobbles
on which high-heeled gull-necked students strode
in March delirious with daffodils,
derivative, underivative. So I say
farewell to the firm colleges and houses,
to the once solid surfaces, to the squat
sacrist in his office, multi-medalled,
also to loud Lorimer, to Law
stout-spectacled and serious in a chair
liquidly lolling.
        O a fond farewell
to all my graveness, my geography
of archway, academe: and archery
of quips, quotations.
                    Unequivocally
I leave the hall, the hallowed hostelry
of a wild openness disorganised.
A fond farewell as I turn northward,
negotiate new currents, wings outspread,
neck long and vulnerable, violate-
goose of the raw spring, not jubilant,
ungregarious guest of the new wind.

Dream

Nervous, I carry my poems
to that chair
from which I read.

Around me
there are men in black masks,
women
with ambiguous laurels.

I speak.
My voice echoes
down the centuries
in competition with, say,
Lucretius.

I lift a huge weight.
My fingers shake,
corrupt compass needles.

O Lord,
let them relent,
smile.
Their harsh faces compose
no images of the rose.

Orpheus,
I am lost among the minerals
of the god of silver.

I rise.
The interview is over.
My poems fly
like the leaves of autumn away
to Vallombrosa.

I cry.
I break like rain
like a fine fresh April
composed of nuns,
shadows.

My masters
are still considering,
among a ring
of rocks and thistles.
Later they will tell me,
much later.

Perhaps when I am no longer here.

The Young Girls

The young girls are waiting to go to university,
they are trembling on the edge of learning.

Donne, Milton, Wordsworth, they are ready to read them.
Poetry has to do with misty mornings

and beginnings, beginnings. Let the toaster click,
let the fridge hum in your new flats

and the book lie open at a page of Marvell's,
while the pale faces dream of love

in the city of buses, chip shops and the underground
where Dido said farewell to Aeneas

as history roared through the tunnels.
                                        How they tremble,
the pages in the fresh wind, as the tenements

echo with the noise of your feet running
to early lectures, and you throw your notes

into the bag carelessly slung over your shoulder.
Beginnings, tremblings... Poetry will move among

the morning shadows. All is transient
nothing is permanent but what will leave later

out of the stone, the books, notes which will tell
what a poem really means, the fixed footnotes.

Tutorial

I went to read to the professor in his house.
He had lost his son in the war.
The trees around the door were luminous,
the noise of the traffic distant. I read
an essay on Cowper to him. He was sparse,
arrogant and cold. His was a tart
curious dryness. (He had written books
on Dante, Leopardi.) Almost as curt
as Dante in his grille of verse he was.
Cowper, he said, don't know him. Really? Did
he praise sofas and tea? I said, Yes.
His head was as imperious as Augustus'.
His son's plane had fallen out of the air.
This was Aberdeen, granitic, bright,
the sea sparkled from mica, and the trees
shaded mysteriously his fine house.
He did not know, I think, of Cowper's madness.
I pitied him profoundly. Nevertheless
he didn't need my pity, shut the door
behind me firmly. Down the avenue
I walked. There was a winding view.
His bony head had gone. The plane rocked
in a scarf of red fire. This was Aberdeen
in '45 and I was seventeen.

Books

Books, what should I do
without you.
I should face
the meagre coarse
board of the world.
But with you,
sombre and true,
I inwardly digest
the rich feast
of learning. Rust
is far from me
as eased by you
I travel through
land after land
in which the gods burned
and the trees rose
shaggy and muscular,
tall and voluptuous,
from whose fine leaves
our pages are made.
O I'm arrayed
in brave dresses,
I am king
when I sit down and bring
your words closer.
Plots, dénouements,
stories and scents,
heroes and saints
these I always find
deep in these fond
gardens of yours –
all literatures.
Nor ever alone
am I, as down
the page my eye races
into your recesses.
Eternal fountains,
lovely philosophies,
brilliant legends,
and dry discourses.
Over-shadowing mountains,

my avid companions
who will not desert
me or my art
with your dry perfume,
calm autumn bloom.
I see my doom
as being always head-bent
over the page
to the very end
like a stone statue
which also has roses.
In the deepest crises
you comfort, you ease –
my allegories!
Tiny mirrors,
and miniature tombs,
you shine in my rooms,
unappeasable ones.
My loves, my true loves,
who will walk through the shades
with me, dear comrades,
without griefs, without griefs.

$$\boxed{5}$$

Others

It is true that there are others . . . of course there are others around
  us,
like the receptionist who has to be patient in her cage,
or the garage mechanic who sets out in pouring rain to repair a car,
or the boy who went to a private school and though he wears
  glasses plays rugby.
Or those who come to poetry readings and who ask no questions
or the gardener who works in the hot day in a cluster of flies
and who peers wistfully into the well where there is no water,
or the male teacher who endures the taunts of children and the
  loveliness of the short-skirted mistress in the staffroom
or the newspaper seller who claps her hands in the bitter cold,
or the librarian who, tired of books, wishes someone would
  speak to her,
or the commissionaire with his blazing medals who stands in the
  evening like a cockerel,
or the waitress who serves at table though her engagement has
  been broken
or the woman who stays with her daughter and son-in-law and
  wishes to be alone
or the blind man who sings songs at an unforgiving corner.
All these there are and do not forget the air they inhabit
as your single will climbs the sky like a jet that's taking off from
  a shining airport
and leaves an ashen mark on a sky of marvellous blue
as it sets off for Canada or Australia or Vietnam or any other
  country
where there are still more of the living centred in their loves and
  their work
and for whom the world is mainly themselves and their own
  shadows
and who stare up at the men with guns and the cold look of the
  tyrant
as the rain falls on the ricefields and on the soaked hats of the
  peasants
and there is autumn somewhere else breathtakingly beautiful
and the apples fall from the trees in the music of the fabulous
  nightingale.

Leaving

How can you imagine
you can begin again
with some forgetful ease,

that you can freely step
with such a large hope
from house to another house,

as if you were a bird,
migrating, unconcerned,
to a fresh land,

leaving its brood behind.
As if unconstrained
by an old mind,

you on spread wings
of love's astonishing
scent should fly off

abrupt, imperative.
What all-forgiving grove
of spring do you sense

without a single fence,
rusted circumference.
To think that life begins

as if the lumpy you
had nothing at all to do
with the first failure,

and that a new colour
as of a yellow dress
or a freshly-ridged blouse

should obliterate the old.
This must be love's wild
folly or good trust,

as recently unhoused
you stand as if new-loosed
in the echoing hall

whose forty years await
your forty years, and light
spreads from small panes

to where you two embrace
with quickly tightening arms,
coiled and lubricious.

In the Evening

Let us drink to the unconsidering evening
as we sit by the window

and the sun is setting.

Let us drink to the wing
of the owl under the weight of darkness.
Let us drink to the stone

as we roll away from this landscape
towards the wall of novels.
Towards the wild head becalmed by sculpture
the cat with the human eyes.

Autumn

The sun shines on my desk.
Such joy, such joy it is
to work as if at music
on such clear autumn days.

When the rowans all in red
bend over water and
above the arranged dead
there is no breath of wind,

and eternity is this
tranquillity and poise
of orange-coloured trees
and flame-red bare displays

as if a visible fire
were an image of itself
both fact and its idea
trembling in double leaf.

Hiding

We know too much about each other. That is why we do not speak.
Our ghosts are buried close together in the one field.
We were once cowards: we were once ridiculous.

And so we don't speak to each other. We do not wish to touch
that skin which is still raw from ridicule
though it has become a victorious flag in a different field.

Insomnia

I wake up in the middle of the night and make a cup of tea.
Because of the fever of my body I can't sleep.

Because of those I've betrayed in the selfishness of my heart
I cannot sleep though the window is open.

I hear the throaty cry of the owl. I imagine its wings,
its body growing greener and greener with horrifying light.

And I remember how a decision was asked of me and I turned
        away,
and climbed the stone steps to my name on the door of my house.

And I shall not sleep till morning and the house will be a glaring
        box
and now and again I will see the rim of a garment

flickering from a bedroom where there has been no one for years.

The Rose Tree

The rose tree stands upright against the wall.
It is our ambition
complete in its unravelled decor.
How perfect, how achieved!
And down below it
there is a frantic foliage,
a boiling of weeds
wishing to be like the tree,
but not powered by its bitter thorns.

In Aberdeen

I listened to you talking about your scripts
and how they were converted into money.

And I remembered how in this city
on a day of silver,
I walked by the cemetery
reciting from *Othello*

'Put up your bright swords
or the dew will rust them.'

Granite and marble
and the silver admirable
northern Venice.

And in the slow river
flowing past the churchyard
a single angler
up to his knees in sparkle.

For Donalda

The swart strait
between us grins
and across it
I hear your cry

O hyacinths of memory
the early sunny
freckled frock,
the mosaic

of our sweet days.
Restlessly I watch the strait
its sweet tranquillity,

the lines of force
I constantly
inscribe, endorse –
that enigmatic lithe sea.

In the Hospital

In the hospital where the women are giving birth
there is a smell of secret milk.

The women thrust their bellies forward
like the prows of proud ships.

Towels, sheets, are everywhere, becalmed sails
with charts of blood on them.

It is a battle to bring a child into the world
from sloping decks and fire.

This hospital is a treasure house, a mint
on which are stamped new souls

deriving from the old ones, full-face, profile,
girls, boys, of a halfway world.

The surgeons hurry past like flying clouds
refreshed by a new breeze,

blue eyes are open like a clutch of eggs
in a nest of white and brown.

Air Hostesses

Air hostesses have a jewelled look
as they rise like us into the sky
among the white hills of clouds
among the shadows of wings.

Who shall hazard such jewels
such waitresses of the infinite.
Who shall on a calm morning
lead them between plain oaks.

They seem too much like angels
for earth to feel their shoes,
for them to speak the words
that will make them equal with flesh.

Give me a glass of orange
or lemon on this fine morning.
Air hostesses, become human,
learn to perspire like us.

Some day your plane will descend
towards a church among fixed trees
and two shadows will walk
towards a large almost safe door.

Capricorn

Capricorn,
my meagre sign,
you shine over my life,

unromantic, thrifty,
cold guest of a sky
without magnificent prizes.

I think of you as the green
wiry sign
of the sparkling intellect,

frugal, exact,
married to the fact
and not the fable,

seduced by enigmas,
and by the many mysteries
of the human mind

which has been designed
beyond the self-contained
stellar light.

Capricorn, spare goat,
you leap in the light
of your own kingdom

cold, gold-coloured,
ambitious and hard
and not feminine,

but sometimes dancing
towards earthy Taurus
in a green ring.

My good masculine sign
I work in your sane
exiguous harmony

with my green pen
dipped in earth and heaven,
one ray among many

and if I suffer ignominy
I still fare forward
into the profound

multifarious glitter,
my wand held in my hand
in a tremble of water.

To a Young Scottish Poet of the Future

In those days, little Scotland will not be enough
with its historical darknesses.

You will learn to visit the world and 'Scotland in relation to it'.

Canada, Australia, Vietnam, they are all waiting.
Your poetry reading may be in a tent
where an Arab drinks sweet coffee.

You will see the jacaranda tree with its purple petals,
you will drink wine with a man who has been in prison
for holding his flag up against the Empire.

Seas you will see, sapphire swimming pools,
over which the bougainvilaea bends.

And you will have to have your pen ready always.

Small Scotland will be a bluebell coloured ring on your finger
from which you will draw sustenance.
It will be your secret bride.

Nevertheless the world opens before you.
Niagara Falls is a voice of the 20th C
with its sharkish waters in which you might drown.

There will be buildings so high that you will not see their tops,
mountains so high that you will not see their summits.

In lobbies of the hotels of the world you will walk,
smiling at people whose language you will not be able to speak.
You will stand among them, a glass of brandy in your hand,
trying to make conversation.

And all the while Scotland will sleep in its history
and the rowan tree will bend over the loch
and there will be moss on an aged gravestone.

But nevertheless you will walk
in the light of contemporary history
where perhaps a gun buckle flashes
and the rose tries to stand ready
in the thunderstorm.

You will stroll at evening over a shaking bridge,
you will stop to give money to beggars,
you will see a white-haired woman in black
carrying a creel.

And the children will hold out their hands mutely
in the universal gesture of poverty
and among the mines of the Golan Heights
you will pick your careful way.

There will be speeches, platitudes, a President will pass in his car,
outriders ahead of him,
and he will wave, and his face is tired above an unrumpled suit.

And you will see the poet who has outlasted his time
haunting hotels, conferences,
hearing ghostly applause
searching for autograph hunters
inviting himself to dinners.

And all the while Scotland and the world will come together,
you will keep it in your wallet
with a few photographs of your children
growing in a distant light.

You will talk to many taxi drivers,
you will sing fados,
you will study in mirrors
your freshly-puzzled face.

Enigmas, revolutions, strange languages,
peasants in carts, wearing their straw hats,
men playing cards in strong sunlight,
the market with its cockerels and fruit.

The peacock too spreading out its marvellous wings,
his plumage of outraged purple,
the horse standing patiently by the roadside,
the shine of a local moon.

It is time for you to enter the world,
its agonies and its anguish,
its strange and brilliant foliage,
the towers of unimaginable heights.

You will travel from airport to airport
seeing the same books at the bookstalls,
and you will hear the voices
of the disembodied captains.

And perhaps one night in Madeira
you will see two lovers hand in hand
among the scent of the jacaranda tree
and you will think:
This is the beginning of things
below the unintelligible words.

Conversion

1
Among the buttercups the breeze strays
over the devout bouquets which crown the desolate tanks.

It was here that the work of the Lord was done
when the hooded enemy scrambled among the stones.

Let us pray, let us remember Masada,
when the Romans built their encampments in the Jewish air.

Solomon is with us, David. The temple is our shade.
Let them animate our arms, the acid smartness of our machine
    guns,

Our children fight for us, switching off their contemporary pop
    songs,
which our bearded black-hatted ones despise, muttering their
    prayers.

This is our land, stones, these are our red roses
which grew on the breasts of the young in the heat of the deserts.

The psalms sing to us, the rivers of Babylon murmur,
we will return from the ghettoes where we hung our lice-infested
    shirts.

In the faces of the Syrians we see the contours of Germans,
we hear the dogs howling on bare peaks without mercy.

Open the Bible in the yellow light of the buttercups,
let us suck from its sustenance, not the graffiti of our days.

Mothers have lullabied their children to these translucent borders.
Boys lie down among flowers so that the prophecies can be fulfilled.

Till the Bible is summoned as reserves,
till the gaunt prophets are mobilised,

till the young boys and young girls surrender their singing,
and exchange their childish bracelets and powder puffs for guns.

We shall hold out against the treacherous ones,
for we are surrounded by foes.

O Lord we are surrounded by enemies, by those who despise us,
who made use of our usury, the shine of our prudent days,

then spat upon our gaberdines, tugged at our beards.
We are besieged by our enemies.

We have lain down and wept, we have begged for our food.
We have chewed our own limbs, they have set dogs upon us.

Now we have set up our bright electronic fence.
No one can touch it without the web being stirred.

Come and save us Lord from the mountains, from the deserts,
when the hooded godless ones speak in barbaric German,

when the skulls dry in the sun, are hung out like washing,
when the Romans come, and the Babylonians and Assyrians
    attack us.

Let us fast in the desert, let us exist on grass,
let us drink the brackish water of exile,

let us sing our songs under the bloodstained moon,
when the animals suck our bones among the cactus.

My young ones, remember the dead, remember Masada,
when you were ceremoniously initiated among the dead

and we became smoke and spirit rather than surrender.
Our gardens are here, this is our country,

this is the land we inherited from the wounded,
from the multiplicity of shoes, bones, badges and teeth,

this is the land, austerely compact of rainbows,
that we dug in the noonday heat, and fructified,

this is the land given to Abraham, to the alert, to the cunning,
this is the country of the arum lily and the Rose of Sharon –

break their bones, destroy them, annihilate the hooded ones,
for we shall fight to the end, we shall chew their armour,

our tanks will strike them in the green fertile valleys,
we shall revenge upon them the injustice of foreign creeds,

and you who have died here shall be immortal,
in our sacred groves we shall carve your eternal names,

and they shall not be ephemeral, as our armour is,
as our bouquets are, as even the cries of the mothers,

for we shall remember you, David, Solomon, Jacob, Esau,
you will be the multifarious foliage of our history,

young ones in your olive green, the flesh of the morning,
the sacrifice whom the Lord abides in his infinite heaven,

the loved ones who shall be the manna of the people,
who shall flourish in the constancy of our marble bibles,

for them we shall pray at the hot wall
bobbing up and down, wearing our shadowy hats,

for Israel is the Chosen One, and it has come to rest
in the serenity of roses and thorns, in our own landscape.

2
Do not believe that we set out without trembling.
Do they set out without trembling?
                              Who can tell?

I carry with me my rifle, my bren gun, the weight of the ages.
My commander is not my sergeant, it is Joshua.

I meet him scanning with his field glasses the contours of the
        Promised Land.
He sits beside a well on an evening of serene pathos.

The same stars attend us, the cries of the children appease us.
The doctors sew in the hospitals their heinous embroidery.

We are the hunchbacks of history. Our wells have been poisoned.
In the cities we have been spat upon, in the courtyards beaten
        with stones.

God has chosen us for punishment, calumny, glory.
We have been worked like plasticine, we are a geometry of thorns.

Our delicate children have been rolled down into pits,
the hiss of the snake has penetrated the ovens.

O Lord when shall we rest, when shall we in the evening
look over our own acres from our luxurious deckchairs.

143

When shall we be able to gaze into our mirrors
without guilt, without venom. When shall our dead lie down

safe from the monsters, gauleiters, the smiles of the evil ones,
the torrent of history which beats on our bare backs.

Profound waters, we have tasted your remoteness.
Profound deserts, we have staggered through your paradoxical
    mirages,

by the light of the Bible, its conspicuous phraseology.
We are not born to be nomads, we are the true inscription of the
    world.

Bring us home to You, destroy our enemies
by this scope that is fixed on that convicted face,

by these planes that compose a serene star of David,
by our haggard and wearisome badges, in the camps without pity.

This is our land, over the grass like the wind,
the voice of the Lord is speaking, our sign and resurrection.

3
In the time of Genesis God made the sun and the stars
and the mellow perfect moon he set over us.

The animals without souls he made in their lithe otherness
(and he set men among the unfading trees).

We from the malarial swamps have created houses:
and vineyards we raised, under the infernal sun.

We have dug and watered, we have made a country suitable for
    Him,
to gaze at in the evening when the day's work is finished.

This is our offering to him, those gardens, these borders,
defended by our sentries, our tanks, from the onset of stones,

the foreign Davids who assumed our personae,
and who would try to beggar us, O Lord, as before,

who would place us again under the hailstones of history,
in the weather of terror, in the bruising eternity of pain.

144

We study in Your name the adamant minutiae
of manuscripts laid open on the steering wheels of our tanks,

and in the hissing conversation of radios we hear You
and see you where the lines cross in our scopes.

The passive one will no longer be passive, O Lord,
we shall set out in the light uniform of warriors,

wearing Your electronic gadgetry, the tribes
whom enemies have summoned from the stained glass windows

into the arena of Your choice, into the stadium,
where we will learn from the Gentiles the obliquities of diplomacy,

and in the tempest we will see You, in the fragrant bouquets
we lay on our tanks, becalmed in the dappled verdure.

4
My father, you told me of the evil that is in some men's eyes,
how on that marvellous summer the train carried you

towards the chambers where the grey snake hissed.
Many died in the music of Beethoven, many newly-clad died,

in the garments of freshness among the unstained tiles.
At first it was woods, then fragrance, their dewy perfumes,

the dapple and silence, then it was orderly men
who seemed just like others absorbed in their poisonous
        documents,

and the sky so clear, so pure – an old man stumbling
laughably somnolent onto the naked platform,

and the trains hissing like snakes. What a clear fresh Eden
after the stink, the sweat, the complaints, the rancours.

This was the grace and the law chiming together
on that morning of air and music, a perfect blue eye,

which we with our rags polluted, our second-rate light.
Theologians, rabbis, lawyers, the web of the mind

confronted by the body tall, perfect, and evil.
We were evil-smelling hunchbacks. History weighed us down,

manuscripts, scansions, lacunae, addenda, corrupted us.
What chance did we have against those who were freshly-born

to the images of reality, to trains just as they were,
to guns just as they were, to the speechless landscape,

to the dew without sorrow, to the bouquets innocent of grief.
What chance did we have, toiling through echoes and Hebrew,

through inconstant mirages, through the repeated theology of pain,
against those who smiled fresh-born in the place where they were.

5
Yes, they were freshly-born to the contours of stones,
to the ravenous heads of dogs, to the shape of syringes,

to the metal of guns, to the mineral gold of teeth.
History opened its gates, and all was permitted.

We on the other hand arrived with our devotion to words
which clouded the world, which misted the pure acts,

legends of law and religion, the fine print of deeds.
We were weighed down with the freight of our symbols.

When shall scholars survive, when shall professors,
when shall financiers survive in the theology of cheques,

when shall scholarship protect us, only the Lord can do that.
But He wished to test us further, we were the sacrifice,

and no fat ram appeared in the thicket to save us.
And no Joseph appeared in the colourful cloak of Egypt.

And no rainbow appeared in the sky, a precious jewel,
but the storm continued in its monotones of brown and of grey.

It was our habit to die, to mislay our addresses,
to be converted to smoke in the languageless air,

where everything was itself, in the eye of the oppressor,
when the trains were themselves, and the ovens and rawness of
    things,

strode without idea startlingly out of the morning,
arrogant, sure and brilliant, extremely themselves,

escaped from morality, from the misty allegiance to language,
from the libraries weighed down with the freight of commentary,

with the work of the skull-capped one who toils through the night,
till he picks up his pen and finds there's a skull on the table,

absolute, peaceful and sure, stripped of idea,
just like a gun in essence, with a hole in the bone.

6

This is our land, visited often by angels,
saved by dreams, visions, cunning, deceit and tactics.

Joseph the dreamer became an arithmetician,
learned a new language to save his people by stealth.

There was force, terror, magic, blood and dementia.
The rod was turned to snake, the snake to a rod.

And the Pharaoh solid as stone floated in robes
through the sky of his godhead but powerless to fight against God,

in an encounter of locusts, frogs, deaths of the first born.
Our God was victorious and random, persistent, omnipotent.

Who are you, angel, arrived among the vernal branches,
tall as a willow in the grass that is bound to fade?

What stupendous message do you bring from the aloof godhead?
The old shall be young, the aged matron give birth.

Even the salt Dead Sea shall be a laboratory of angels
and over infernal Sodom your hand shall be stretched.

Pillars of salt and fire, clouds compact of thunder,
the snakes of venomous light shall be set in the sky,

the desert will flourish, there will be human deception,
and the Lord will work out the judgment of his books,

the finances of his balances, His credits of mercy.
The angels will climb up and down on his glittering ladder

and the Lord will read off the configurations of his radar
and direct his guns towards foes in remorseless arcs.

7
Lord, I am waiting. Here is your perfect servant.
The breeze strays through the grass, the morning is cool.

I belong to the army of spirits that surrounds me.
On the mountain ahead of me, that bush is brilliant red,

an immortal poppy cleansed of ambiguous grief.
Our planes are travelling eastward towards the sun.

I belong to the hosts of God, invisible, pious.
My tunic sweats a little in this temporal wind

as once perhaps Joshua's seeing the land before him,
promised and dear. There is no undivided morning,

each is a bead hung on a historical chain.
Each is sacred with deeds, forgiven by justice,

the language of God is eternal, is Hebraic.
It is the black shadow cast on the steel of that tank.

Listen, I stand at attention before God,
the hum of his voice is persistent in my headphones

as the hum of that bee over that luminous flower.
Remember their hosts, their armies, their rancorous journey,

the wells where the angels bent down as into mirrors
to study their faces, imprints of passionate God.

I am ready, resolved. How shall the heart be passive
doglike or servile? God springs from the clouds,

eternal athlete, soldier, militant actor.
Soon I shall hear His voice, ardent and pure.

8
In the battle, furious and fierce, we held them.
Our predestined rainbows of fire homed on their tanks.

They blossomed afresh in the vernal airs of the morning.
What was their diurnal shelter in the anger of God?

In the banality of light they keeled to the fading grass.
We read off the abstract measurements which destroyed them.

O Lord we see You in the mysterious agreement of numbers,
in the hallowed coordinates, in the blossoms of regular fire,

the parishes of death, of the quick and fiery poppies,
the drifting bushes of smoke. The armoured crabs

scuttled in a sea of green, nervous, ingenious.
We held them, Lord, this day, till Your reserves

of Bibles and laws were quickly summoned to help us.
The grey flowers rose and dwelt on Your holy slopes,

and these were Your voices, these clouds of thunder and light
ascending, descending. O Lord, you laughed

among the trumpets ha ha. Whose was that laughter?
Was it mine or Yours? Exaltation and terror

were together in tether. Handcuffed they rode
into the arena of grief, jubilation.
                                        Once I saw

a face, not yet dead, behind an exploding window.
I was close, so close, I didn't wish it so close,

a boy's face, my own. Was it reflection or presence?
A brief temporal profile, it passed in the storm.

9
All is quiet now, though the battle's not finished.
I can almost hear the fall of the dew on the grass.

Your triumphant moon strides the harmonious heavens.
Some tanks are becalmed among Your mirages of light.

You have put out Your hand, I saw it, mailed and unclouded,
though all is now quiet under the sparkles of dew

which falls on the bodies, the private statuesque faces.
Mordecai lies there, Isaac, Joseph lies there,

in this immaculate light. How can I sleep?
I am tortured by exquisite joy, by choking excitement,

I am surrounded by spirits. Moses, you walk
down from the mountains, Your cloak disfigured by bullets.

an astrology of deaths has embroidered Your disfigured coat.
And, also I see you walking among the bodies,

dishonoured Absalom. Here are the phantom tribes
bearing the Ark, swaying among the bodies,

this moonlight, David, is the yellow strings of your harp,
the roads the Assyrians took. Nocturnal manna,

of vapour and dew, I hear you steadily fall,
I hear you so clearly, a river falling from heaven,

and the faces are delicate imprints, the faces of the dead.
I walk without sleep, I haunt, O Lord, Your tents.

10
So pure these faces like petals. Who would have known?
Even the enemy dead in their concentration

are like flowers of Lebanon, like the petals of Sharon.
The Bible was their target; see, it is holed with their bullets,

its absolute words are drenched in this cold dew.
I am the ancient scholar bent over the dead,

chanting, reciting. Always the prophets are crying.
God has been replaced by history, by events,

and events are God. Whatever is happening happens,
and must be explained as God, our terror, our swords,

these are explained as God's inflexible judgment.
The armies are God's, the rainbows, the out-pulled teeth,

the scholar beaten to death by his own volumes,
the torturer's scholarly face, his fanatic corrections,

these too are God's. That is the lie, the lie.
How shall events and God be made synonymous

except to explain the exile and the grief,
except to explain the trains, and now the tanks,

except to explain my trembling, a petal of God's,
this trembling at night. The morning light hasn't broken,

but all has been named. Adam too was event,
and Eve's sharp teeth sunk in the shining apple,

and the furious web he made of astronomy, earth,
theology, mathematics: the excessive and spectral web

from the meagre fruit and the grass. I see it shine.
Event, event, and then the furious maze

woven so intricately over the frightening chasm,
the whole earth become a fine ideology

humming and buzzing in which the skulls are enmeshed.
This silence appals. Out of the lion the honey,

and out of the honey the lion with strong white teeth.
Events, events, the programme of serious Jehovah,

the honeyed web of the planets fixed in their pose.
We who are finite have wrestled with the infinite,

out of our own bones made God, from our longing bones.
And he strides belligerently now about our tents

satanic and furious and cunning. We have made God,
The stone hits Goliath, his armour falls to the ground.

a brilliant futile cobweb. We've made Goliath.
See, his armour is peeling. His eye is a stone.

11
I bend and touch you, my enemies in the dawn.
Somewhere in this light the Idea explodes,

and rules, commandments, tablets, are blown away.
This grass appals our hitherto holy logic,

the minutiae of our testaments. I am here
alone, unsacred, in these early mists

swirling about my head. The sun will burn
soon like an armoured head. It is not God

nor our history's red helmet. It's the sun,
not jubilant or just, but the fire

natural in its socket of routine,
unwithering and distant. We shall soon

advance in our ponderous chains, prisoners
of symbol and of language, echoing forth

the voices of our power.
                              We should not be
denunciatory prophets in this light

falling so helplessly around us all,
even on our enemies, now dead,

in their lucidity of pathos. Now it is,
the tents are lightening. It is time to stand

among these misty armies, it is time
not to defend the indefensible. We were mazed

by the heroes of our childhood. But the dream
of trumpets fades. I was caught

in a ruinous snare of history and books.
Now however there are human eyes

staring at me in this light and dew,
even my enemies. I'm a voyeur

of final uncluttered pure humanity.
I tremble like a leaf, I am freed

of symbol and of language. All I see
is Death the horse nibbling with stony teeth.